Mythical Beasts

MIGHTY MUTANTS

Thanks to the creative team:
Senior Editor: Matthew Rake
Designer: Lauren Woods and collaborate agency

Original edition copyright 2015 by Hungry Tomato Ltd.

Hungry Tomato™
A division of Lerner Publishing Group, Inc.
241 First Avenue North
Minneapolis, MN 55401 USA

For reading levels and more information, look up this title
at www.lernerbooks.com.

Main body text set in Galahad Std 12/1.5
Typeface provided by Adobe Systems.

The Cataloging-in-Publication Data for *Mighty Mutant*s is on file at
the Library of Congress.

ISBN 978-1-4677-6343-1 (lib. bdg.)
ISBN 978-1-4677-7652-3 (pbk.)
ISBN 978-1-4677-7216-7 (EB pdf)

Manufactured in the United States of America
1 – VP – 7/15/15

Mythical Beasts

MIGHTY
MUTANTS

By Alice Peebles

Illustrated by Nigel Chilvers

HUNGRY
TOMATO™

Minneapolis

"As battle raged, the massive wolf
Fenrir howled with a thundering menace.
'Ragnarok, doom of the gods, has
co-o-o-ome,' sounded his chilling cry. This
was his hour for revenge. None other than
mighty god Odin was striding toward him,
whirling his spear, Gungnir."

Contents

Mighty Mutants

Meet the ten fiercest, most strangely shaped mythical beings ever. These supernatural beasts are like no animals you've seen before . . .

Thunderbird, a figure of American Indian myths, and the Chinese deity Lei Gong rule the heavens. The sky also holds fiery Surt, who led his fire giants into the last great battle against the Norse gods and consumed their world with flames. And Indian mythology tells of the golden-winged bird Garuda, who can swallow whole rivers. Other hybrid creatures live in the seas or roam the earth.

Many of these mutants are the offspring of gods. They have supernatural strength and enormous size. This is true of the monstrous wolf Fenrir, as well as the Midgard Serpent, which grew large enough to encircle the entire world and hold its tail in its mouth. But how did the hideous Grendel come to haunt the Anglo-Saxon world? All that those ancient Danish warriors know is that he likes to feast on their blood!

So which of these creatures is the most powerful? You're about to find out.

The ten beasts are shown in vivid scenes that are based on particular moments in their stories . . . perhaps struggling with a hated enemy or swallowing helpless mortals. The details about each monster are inspired by mythology and folklore handed down since ancient times. The creatures appear in ranked order from least to most powerful, with scores from 1 through 10 for each of five categories: Strength, Repulsiveness, Special Powers, Ferocity, and Invincibility. You'll also find a suggestion on how to defeat or neutralize each one . . . though you may decide it's best just to run for cover!

Hold on tight as you sail into the dangerous waters of the Kraken and Leviathan, or battle alongside Zeus against the vengeful, rock-spitting monster Typhon. Keep your nerve and keep on reading to find out more about these powerful beasts.

Great Bird of the Sun
Garuda

When he stretched out his wings, he seemed to fill the sky, and they were so shimmeringly bright that mortals thought they were the rays of the sun itself. Garuda was on a mission: to steal the elixir of immortality, the amrita, from the gods.

Noiselessly as a leaf he glided to the highest mountain peak in the heavens, where fire-spitting serpents guarded the precious fluid. Feeling an unusual wind overhead, they rose up to attack. Garuda raised a dust storm that blinded the serpents and choked their fire. They collapsed on the ground in a confused tangle, while Garuda whirled away, the pot of amrita in his talons.

How to defeat Garuda

It would take some mean trickery indeed to outdo this cool operator. Since much of his power lies in his mighty wings, he would need to be lulled by a sleeping potion so that his giant feathers could be removed, one by one.

Where does this myth come from?

In Hindu mythology, Garuda is the charioteer of the god Vishnu. He stole the sacred nectar as a ransom for his mother, Vinata, who was imprisoned by her sister. Garuda features in the Indian epic poem, the Mahabharata, *written beginning in 400 BCE. More than 1,000 years before that he appears as the eagle in sacred texts called the Vedas.*

Beast
Power

Strength
10

Repulsiveness
0

Special Powers
3

Ferocity
4

Invincibility
8

Total
25/50

Lord of Thunder
Lei Gong

Squealing and whimpering, the two demons darted here and there as thunder rolled overhead. They knew what that meant. Lei Gong! Their thought turned into a vision. Looking up, they could see his wings and clawed feet. He circled overhead, crashing his mallet on his drum.

"This is for terrorizing an old lady and stealing her tiny collection of coins!" Lei Gong accompanied his words with the loudest crash on his drum. It was no use covering their ears and running away. The demons staggered and fell, feeling that their heads would split as their evil deeds came back to torment them.

How to defeat Lei Gong

The best plan would be to avoid the attention of the mighty god, who punishes those who behave cruelly. So humans have to try and behave well toward one another. For demons, this is more difficult, since they're naturally cruel . . .

Where does this myth come from?

Lei Gong is a deity in the ancient Chinese religious tradition of Taoism, which emphasizes compassion and humility. Whenever a mortal commits a crime or a demon harms a mortal on Earth, Lei Gong is sent down from heaven with his mallet, drum, and chisel to make thunder and punish them.

Beast Power

Strength
8

Repulsiveness
3

Special Powers
1

Ferocity
8

Invincibility
7

**Total
27/50**

Night Prowler
Grendel

Many, many times he had torn apart the limbs of good Danish warriors and splashed their blood about the king's honey wine hall. Now as he trudged across the moor from his lair, Grendel smelled a new human scent on the air. This night, Beowulf and his brave heroes were sleeping in the hall. Smashing down the door, Grendel grabbed the first warrior in his clawed hand . . . and gulped him down. With cries of horror and fury, the others grabbed their swords and hacked at his legs. Then Beowulf stepped up . . .

How to defeat Grendel

Beowulf vanquishes Grendel by clinging to him and wearing him out in a long, drawn-out combat. He tears off one of Grendel's arms, and Grendel returns to his lair to die.

Where does this myth come from?

The tale of Grendel occurs in the long poem Beowulf, *named after its hero and written in Anglo-Saxon, or Old English. It probably dates from the eighth century CE. Other episodes in the poem include Beowulf's battles with Grendel's mother, who wants revenge, and with a giant sea serpent.*

Beast Power

Strength
7

Repulsiveness
6

Special Powers
0

Ferocity
8

Invincibility
7

Total
28/50

Odin's Nemesis
Fenrir

It was the time of reckoning for the gods and giants of the remote northern realms. As battle raged, the massive wolf Fenrir bayed menacingly, "Ragnarok, doom of the gods, has co-o-o-ome!" This was his hour for revenge. None other than mighty god Odin was striding toward him, whirling his spear, Gungnir.

Swollen with fury, Fenrir leapt to his feet and burst the magic chain that had bound him for so many years. Towering over Odin, he scooped up the god and gulped him down with a howl of glee. The final destiny of Odin, father of all the gods, was complete.

How to defeat Fenrir

One version of the tale relates that after Odin's defeat, Vidar, the half-god, half-giant son of Odin, avenged his father's death. Using his great strength, he pulled Fenrir's jaws apart and tore the monster in two.

Where does this myth come from?

Fenrir is one of the most important and fearsome creatures in Norse mythology. His story occurs in a famous source for the Norse myths, the Prose Edda, *written in the thirteenth century. These tales were arranged and recounted by the Icelandic historian Snorri Sturluson, who studied the ancient beliefs of the early Scandinavian peoples.*

Beast Power

Strength
9

Repulsiveness
2

Special Powers
0

Ferocity
10

Invincibility
8

Total
29/50

Storm Spirit
Thunderbird

For weeks, winds and rain lashed the land. Hailstones the size of fists smashed crops and fruit into the ground, while the fertile hinterland became a muddy swamp. There was no fishing, no hunting, no food. The chief called on the Great Spirit for help. His desperate people waited.

Then one evening, the clouds lit up with a dazzling wall of lightning. A huge bird, pitch black against the brightness, powered toward the waiting people. In its talons it held a gigantic . . . fish? The bird lowered its gift to the ground. It was a whale. As the people gazed in wonder and gratitude, Thunderbird soared away into the storm.

How to defeat Thunderbird

Thunderbird's preferred prey is the whale, and only such a huge creature might possibly thwart him. A whale once did put up such a fight that trees were torn up and mountains shaken, so Thunderbird finally had to give up the struggle.

Where does this myth come from?

This story is told by the Quileute people, whose land was along the northwestern coast of the United States, in what is now Washington State. The Quileute were skilled boatbuilders and fishermen, as well as whale and seal hunters. Belief in Thunderbird as an elemental spirit is widespread among many other American Indian peoples.

Beast Power

Strength
9

Repulsiveness
0

Special Powers
6

Ferocity
7

Invincibility
8

Total
30/50

Girdle of the World
The Midgard Serpent

The giant Hymir watched uneasily as Thor baited his fishing line with an ox's head and dropped it into the sea. Now Hymir turned white as the sea boiled like a cauldron and a huge serpent's head rose streaming from the waves.

"Ha, you liked my ox's head!" laughed Thor. He aimed his hammer, Mjollnir, at the serpent's skull, just as Hymir flung himself forward and cut the fishing line. With a glance of hatred at Thor, the serpent disappeared underwater.

)•●•(

How to defeat the Midgard Serpent

At Ragnarok, the final battle of the Norse gods, Thor again meets the Midgard Serpent, who fights alongside the giants. Thor slays him with Mjollnir, his hammer.

Beast Power

Strength
10

Repulsiveness
4

Special Powers
2

Ferocity
7

Invincibility
8

Total
31/50

Where does this myth come from?

This tale of Norse mythology occurs in the thirteenth-century Prose Edda *compiled by the poet Snorri Sturluson. Earlier versions exist in poems of the Viking era. The story was even carved on pictorial stones around 1050. One image shows Thor with his feet pushed right through the bottom of the boat and the serpent hooked on his line.*

Tentacled Devourer
The Kraken

"Land ahoy!" shouted the first mate. The captain swept the choppy sea with his telescope. Ahead was a small, rocky island.

The next moment, the ship started rolling. Men slithered from one side of the deck to the other. The island was heaving up from the water, creating a storm of blinding spray. A spiked head as large as the ship itself emerged. Huge tentacles thrashed about, toppling the ship this way and that, until one tentacle lifted it right up in the air toward that hideous mouth . . .

How to defeat the Kraken

Defeat might not be possible, but firing explosives down its gullet could make the Kraken back off.

Beast Power

Strength
9

Repulsiveness
7

Special Powers
0

Ferocity
7

Invincibility
9

Total
32/50

Where does this myth come from?

Tales of the many-armed Kraken originate mainly from twelfth-century Norse literature. A similar horned, black sea monster was described by the Swedish historian Olaus Magnus in 1555. Belief in the Kraken is probably based on sightings of the aggressive but rarely seen giant squid, a deep ocean dweller that really does exist.

King of the Fire Giants
Surt

Warrior cries and death groans, thunder and lightning filled the air as gods and giants clashed at Ragnarok. Now a dark shape descended from the sky . . . dark, but brandishing a burning sword. It was Surt, bringer of fire, who roared out one name: "Frey!"

Armed with only a deer's antler, Frey the fair-weather god met his fiery opponent. For an hour, he dodged Surt's flaming weapon, which scorched his skin and hair, while he jabbed and aimed blows with the pointed antler. Finally Frey dived under the giant's sweeping arm, and even as the flames burned him, he pierced Surt through the heart.

How to defeat Surt

An opponent who is not a god would have to contain Surt's fires by starving them of air. Perhaps the giant could be lured to an underground cavern and with all entrances and air vents sealed. There he could smolder away without causing harm.

Where does this myth come from?

Surt, whose name means black, is a character of Norse mythology mentioned in tenth-century poems and the later Prose Edda of Snorri Sturluson. His continuing association with the volcanic hotspot of Iceland is shown in the names of its mile-long lava cave, Surtshellir, and the island of Surtsey.

3

Beast
Power

Strength
9

Repulsiveness
2

Special Powers
6

Ferocity
9

Invincibility
8

Total
34 /50

Challenger of Zeus
Typhon

Olympus shook as chunks of mountain and gobs of molten rock hit it from base to summit: deadly missiles flung from the powerful hands and fiery mouth of Typhon. All the gods fled except for Zeus and Athena, his fearless warrior daughter. Zeus hurled thunderbolts and an unbreakable sickle that stuck in Typhon's flesh, so that his massive body bled from many wounds.

Though weakening, he entwined the god in his coils, and they rolled around the slopes of Olympus in a fight to the death. Typhon wrenched the sickle free and cut out the sinews of mighty Zeus, leaving him flopping on the ground . . .

How to defeat Typhon

Only Zeus could do this. With the help of Pan and Hermes, he once more does battle. Blasting Typhon with thunderbolts, he buries him below the island of Sicily. Sometimes Typhon's breath filters up from the earth through bubbling Mount Etna.

Where does this myth come from?

The largest and strongest giant of Greek mythology, Typhon was the son of Gaia, the goddess of Earth. At the time, Zeus and the gods of Olympus were establishing their supremacy in the universe. Gaia wanted to punish them for defeating the earthborn giants, and she sent her son to do the task.

Beast
Power

Strength
9

Repulsiveness
7

Special Powers
4

Ferocity
10

Invincibility
9

Total
39/50

Deepsea Horror
Leviathan

For days the ship had lain calm on the glassy ocean. At last, a puff of cloud appeared, shaped by a freshening wind. Now the ship scudded along.

The sea began washing over the deck. Each wave was larger than the last, and one shattered the masts. The men who had been so silent now cried out in terror.

An abyss had opened up ahead. The ship lurched helplessly toward it, and the men just had time to see fire-filled nostrils and rows of towering teeth before they slipped into the darkness . . .

How to defeat Leviathan

The only chance might be to blind the beast with flares and then escape. They would need to be fired from a safe distance.

Beast Power

Strength
10

Repulsiveness
8

Special Powers
3

Ferocity
10

Invincibility
10

Total
41/50

Where does this myth come from?

The idea of an enormous, all-powerful sea serpent existed in the ancient mythologies of Canaan and Babylon, now roughly the area of Israel, Lebanon, Syria, and Iraq. One story tells how the fertility god Baal killed Lotan, or Leviathan, which was described as a seven-headed sea dragon.

Rogues' Gallery

10

Garuda

In order to steal the sacred nectar, Garuda also had to put out fires surrounding the mountains where it was kept. He did this by pouring the world's rivers over the flames.

9

Lei Gong

The thunder deity is winged, with a man's body (often colored blue), and with a curved beak. His wife, Tian Mu, creates lightning with flashing mirrors.

6

Thunderbird

In many myths, Thunderbird has no obvious bodily shape but instead has the form and substance of clouds, with a beak but no head, talons, or feet.

5

The Midgard Serpent

A monstrous child of the god-giant Loki and the giantess Angrboda, he was thrown into the seas and grew large enough to circle the entire world.

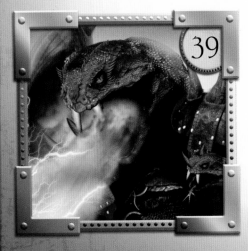

2

Typhon

Typhon grew so huge that it was said he could wade through the sea, while his head brushed the stars. He is described as having either multiple snake or animal heads, each mouth with a voice of its own: a bellowing bull, a roaring lion, or a howling wolf. Serpents coiled around his body, and his hands ended in snakes instead of fingers.

8
Grendel
In two early raids, Grendel killed all the Danish lords. This began his twelve-year reign of terror over the Danish people before he met Beowulf.

7
Fenrir
The son of the half-god, half-giant Loki and a giantess, Angrboda, Fenrir spent many years chained up by the gods, which made him thirsty for revenge.

4
The Kraken
According to one description, sailors were in danger of being sucked down by the whirlpool created when the Kraken sank back down to the sea.

3
Surt
Surt leads a band of troops against the gods at Ragnarok. The firestorms that end the battle by destroying the world are known as Surtalogi or Surt's Fire.

1
Leviathan
Destructive and relentless, like the ocean it inhabited, Leviathan was thought to cause raging seas and even tsunamis. It had an outer layer of scales, hard as steel, that no sharp weapon could penetrate. It was often described as horned, fire-breathing, and multiheaded.

Want to Know More?

The Wrath of Fenrir

The Norse gods knew that their fate was linked to the gigantic wolf, Fenrir, so to keep him under their control they raised him from puppyhood. But as he kept growing larger and stronger, they began to fear him, and only Tyr the war god had the courage to go near enough to feed him.

Fenrir burst two chains of the gods' making before they presented him with the light and silken Gleipnir. This fine, soft fetter had been made by dwarf magic from nonexistent ingredients, such as the sound of a cat's footfall, the roots of stones, and the breath of a fish. It was impossibly strong. Fenrir, suspecting a trick, refused to try it unless a god put his hand in his mouth, and once more brave Tyr stepped up to the mark.

As the chain was slipped on, Fenrir struggled uselessly and in a fury bit off Tyr's hand: a disastrous injury for a god of battle. The gods transported Fenrir to a desolate place and tied the chain to a boulder. His jaws were propped open with a sword and the foam from his furious howling poured down on Earth to form a river.

The Final Battle

As time went by, the mischief-making god Loki (who was also part giant) became a nasty nuisance and then a serious danger to the Norse gods, powerful as they were. His ultimate crime was to cause the death of Baldur, one of Odin's sons and a much-loved god. After this, the gods chained him up in a dark cavern (as they had chained his son Fenrir) and a serpent dripped poison from overhead, causing him to writhe in agony.

At Ragnarok, Loki broke free from his fetters and summoned the Frost and Fire Giants from their different realms, signaling the final battle between gods and giants. Odin's ever-watchful son Heimdall, guardian of the gods' stronghold, Asgard, was the first to spot the arrival of these fearsome hordes. He boomed out a warning on his horn, and at once the gods knew that their destiny was at hand. Heimdall himself was killed by Loki.

Raging to bring about the gods' downfall, Fenrir joined the throng, while Loki's other offspring, the Midgard Serpent, rose up from the ocean, causing a deluge on land. As the Serpent slithered over the rainbow bridge into Asgard, it collapsed, and the gods' stronghold became the scene of a battle to end all battles. Ragnarok demolished Asgard and the entire cosmos, but a new world came into being in which some gods survived and some were reborn.

Storm Makers and Creators

Many American Indian peoples believed that Thunderbird caused storms by beating his wings and lightning by blinking his eyes. There were many thunderbirds, although all were ruled by the Great Thunderbird, which was one of four elders. The others were the Red Thunderbird of the north, the Yellow Thunderbird of the west, and the White Thunderbird of the south. They lived in a backward-rotating dimension, the opposite of the clockwise movement of Earth.

Some cultures thought thunderbirds were the ancestors of humans. Others said that thunderbirds were linked to the creation of the world itself. They were often seen as the enemies of snakes. One Lakota myth tells that the Wakinyan (thunderbirds) battled the monstrous water spirits called the Unktehi that lived in the Missouri River. These had flooded the land to drown the first humans, thinking they were lice. The battle continued for many ages, with the thunderbirds fighting on the side of humans. They won by shooting down thunderbolts from high overhead, scorching the earth and drying up the water spirits' flesh. All that remained were giant bones . . . just like the fossils of giant mosasaurs, marine reptiles of the Cretaceous period, found in the Badlands of South Dakota.

Index

The Author

Alice Peebles is an editor and writer specializing in the arts and humanities for children. She is a coauthor of *Encyclopedia of Art for Young People* and one of the creators of *The Guzunder Gang* audiobook series. She has also edited and written for several children's magazines focused on history, art, geography. She lives in London, England.

The Artist

Nigel Chilvers is a digital illustrator based in the United Kingdom. He has illustrated numerous children's books.